P9-BIX-653

My Harvest Home

*A Celebration of Polish
Songs, Dances, Games and Customs*

*Thanks for all
your love & support.
Andrea & Peter*

My Harvest Home

*A Celebration of Polish
Songs, Dances, Games and Customs*

Andrea Schafer

Illustrated by Peter Schafer

World Music Press

My Harvest Home
A Celebration of Polish
Songs, Dances, Games and Customs

by Andrea Schafer
Illustrated by Peter Schafer

© 1995 Andrea Schafer/World Music Press
Illustrations © 1995 Peter Schafer
Published by World Music Press
P.O. Box 2565 Danbury CT 06813-2565 (203) 748-1131

Judith Cook Tucker, Publisher, Editor-in-Chief
Claudia Chapman, Graphic Designer, Associate Editor

No part of this work or its companion recording may be reproduced in any form or by any means
except for short excerpts in reviews, without permission in writing from the publisher.
The map and selected individual musical transcriptions may be copied for use with students
by the purchaser, at a single site, so long as the copyright information, title, author's name
and the phrase "Used by permission" is included on each copy.

ISBN 0-937203-68-8 Book/audio cassette SET
ISBN 0-937203-69-6 Book/CD SET

Original paperback edition
Printed in the United States of America on acid-free paper
1 2 3 4 5 6 7 8 9

Music engraved by Don Wallace using Finale ®
Book and cover design by Claudia Chapman using Reacy, Set, Go! 6.0 ®
Cover and inside art © 1995 by Peter Schafer
Dance Photographs © 1995 Ann and Grant Geisert
Portrait of Andrea and Peter Schafer by Root Photographers, Inc.
Other photos by Andrea Schafer © 1995, except as noted
Library of Congress Cataloging-in-Publication Data
LC95-

Acknowledgements
I'd like to thank the following for their guidance and help:
My husband Peter
My mother Wanda Kabala
My in-laws Chet and Dolores Schafer
Lucyna Migala
Anthony and Sabina Dobrzanski
Ada Dziewanowska
Paula Kowalkowski
Beata Borawska
The Lira Ensemble for use of costumes
Polish National Tourist Office of Chicago for photos of Poland
Ann and Grant Geisert for dance photography
Tom Schafer, recording engineer
The following musicians:
Diane Busko Bryks
Stanley and Chester Pytlik
John Makowka
Andrew Bocek

Contents

Transcriptions

About The Author

Andrea and Peter Schafer

*A*ndrea Schafer is a third generation Polish-American whose four grandparents, seeking better lives for themselves, came to the United States during the Great Immigration in the early 1900s. She was introduced to Polish songs, stories, and traditions by her grandparents who never quite mastered English. Her parents were born in Chicago, IL. They spoke Polish in their homes, but her father lost most of the language. (As was the case with many children of immigrants, he wanted to speak English.) Her mother, a fluent Polish speaker, wanted to pass on the Polish language and traditions. Between the ages of seven through ten, Andrea was enrolled at a Polish Saturday school sponsored by the Polish National Alliance of America. Each week she received one hour of language instruction, one hour of folk and traditional songs, and one hour of folk dancing. This organization gave her many opportunities to perform children's folk dances and nurtured a love of the music and dances that grew over the years.

Andrea holds a bachelors degree in music education from DePaul University, a masters degree in vocal performance from the American Conservatory of Music, and Orff-Schulwerk certification. She is a music teacher at the elementary level in Highland Park, a suburb of Chicago. She has journeyed to Poland five times, to visit family and explore her cultural roots. She has performed Polish national and folk dances with the Polonez Dancers and has performed with the Lira Ensemble since 1976 as a singer and dancer. Established in 1965, this is the only professional organization in the United States that performs Polish music of all genres. It brings Polish music and dance into American life and builds bridges of understanding through presentations of Polish culture. It has made six recordings and traveled on six concert tours of Poland. Its Artistic Director and General Manager is Lucyna Migala. The choreographer is Anthony Dobrzanski.

Through her performing, Andrea met her husband, Peter, also a third generation Polish-American, a dancer, and folk artist. Together, they continue to learn, love, and perform songs and dances of Poland.

About The Artist

$\mathcal{P}$eter Schafer was born in the United States. All of his grandparents came from Poland during the Great Immigration. His grandfather's name was originally Szafraniec, but because it was difficult for a Pole to get a job in a primarily German district of Chicago, his grandfather changed the name to its current form.

Peter is a biochemist, but has loved Polish folk art since he was a boy. He began cutting wycinanki around the age of nine when he saw his older sisters doing it. It has become an area of interest and a hobby for him ever since. His tools of choice are not sheep shears, but a good pair of scissors, colored paper, and rubber cement.

About The Performers

The Pytlik Brothers Polish Folk Ensemble of Chicago
Chester Pytlik, accordion
Stanley Pytlik, clarinet
Andrew Bocek, violin
John Makowka, string bass

$\mathcal{T}$he members of this ensemble were born in Poland where learning to play instruments was a family tradition. Relatives passed on their knowledge of the instruments and encouraged them as young boys to play together first by ear, and later by musical notation. In the 1970s they moved to Chicago, Illinois and continue the tradition playing for various dance groups and traveling throughout the United States. One can hear the authenticity that twenty to thirty years of performing together brings.

About The Singer

$\mathcal{D}$iane Busko Bryks, mezzo-soprano, is a second generation Polish-American. She studied at the Chicago Conservatory College of Music, Northwestern and DePaul Universities, and at the American Institute of Musical Studies in Graz, Austria. For more than ten years, Ms. Busko Bryks has been a professional member of the Chicago Symphony Chorus, where she has also worked as soloist and has understudied major roles. She is a singer with the Lira Ensemble and serves as vocal coach for the ensemble. She has performed with the *Oak Park Civic Opera, the Lithuanian Opera Company of Chicago, the Halevi Choral Society,* and *the Oriana Singers.* Ms. Busko Bryks holds a degree in Music Education and is a music teacher at the elementary level in La Grange, Illinois.

Introduction

*M*y Harvest Home is a heartfelt collection of some of my favorite songs, dances, games, sayings and customs from a variety of regions and seasons. It includes historical and cultural background about Poland and the Polish-American community, as well as musical selections suitable for all ages and abilities. The recipes are widely known and well loved—sustenance for our journey. The folkart projects will brighten your environment and create a setting for the music. It is my intent to share with you a taste of Poland's cultural richness, and to provide a springboard to set your students' imaginations in motion, to enhance your music or social studies curriculum, or simply to guide you to a greater appreciation of the heritage of so many Americans. There is far more to Polish music and dance than the polka. My homelife taught me that early on, and my many trips to my family's homeland made it even more clear. It is my pleasure to share my musical "journal" with you.

cousins from Ryglice

Gdańsk Old Town

A Visit To My HOMELAND

Gdańsk Photo Courtesy of Polish National Tourist Office

Family ABROAD

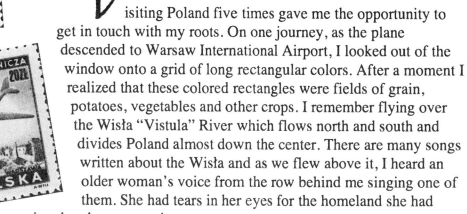

Visiting Poland five times gave me the opportunity to get in touch with my roots. On one journey, as the plane descended to Warsaw International Airport, I looked out of the window onto a grid of long rectangular colors. After a moment I realized that these colored rectangles were fields of grain, potatoes, vegetables and other crops. I remember flying over the Wisła "Vistula" River which flows north and south and divides Poland almost down the center. There are many songs written about the Wisła and as we flew above it, I heard an older woman's voice from the row behind me singing one of them. She had tears in her eyes for the homeland she had missed and was returning to.

My family is from the southeastern region of Poland known as the Rzeszów Region, and live in the agricultural villages of Kolbuszowa, Ryglice and Żołków. These villages are in the midst of the rolling foothills at the base of the Carpathian mountains. On my last trip to Poland in 1994, I had the opportunity to travel by bus through this entire region and finally realized what my grandmothers were·so homesick for. Green and gold fields spotted with haystacks and sunflowers, flower and vegetable gardens, were everywhere. The road is rarely straight, but winds up and down the gently rolling hills. Turn the corner and yet another breathtaking view appears. There is nothing in the United States that can compare with this old world charm and abundant richness of the land. This is the Poland my grandparents loved and remembered, this is the Poland that I love and remember.

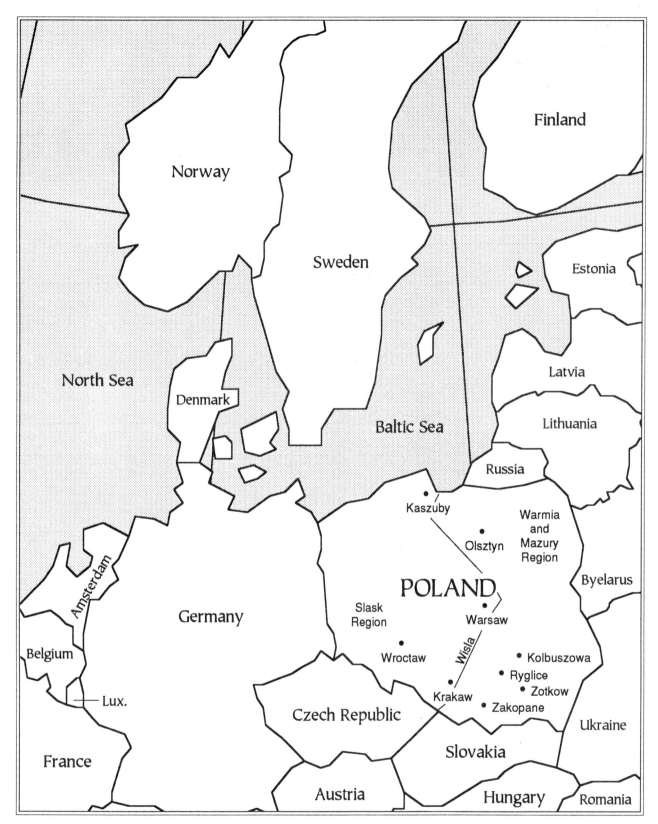

POLAND

A Brief HISTORY

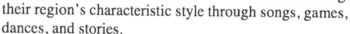

Poland is a country where people have always expressed themselves through song and dance in a wide range of styles reflecting the country's rich history and culture. This richness is due in part to Poland's regional differences. With the Baltic Sea on the north, Carpathian mountains on the south, Bielorus and the Ukraine on the east, and Germany on the west, it is no wonder that there are more than thirty different regions. Over the centuries, each region has developed its own unique musical style, characteristic dances, and colorful costumes. Children in Poland are taught their region's characteristic style through songs, games, dances, and stories.

The word Poland comes from the Polish word *pole* (POH-leh) which means field. Dating back to 1900 B.C., the area around the *Wisła* (VEE-swah) and *Warta* (VAHR-tah) rivers was inhabited by different Slavic tribes. They were primarily self-contained tribes that developed their own characteristic style. The Polabian tribe in particular remained in this area and worked the land. The first documented rulers were of the Piast Dynasty which began in 840 A.D. In the 1100s, Poland was divided into principalities which were then ruled by different nobles. (In 1386, Queen Jadwiga of Poland married Jagiello, a Grand Duke of Lithuania, and united both countries. This vast empire stretched across most of central Europe and remained under one rule for over two hundred years.)

In 966, Poland became Christianized and allied itself with the Roman Catholic Church. This relationship has remained very strong even to this day. Church music influenced the previously five tone scale to assume a Western modality. Because it follows Western practices, much of Poland's music sounds very conforming and not very unusual to Western ears. It is when the listener explores the regional differences that Turkish, Ukranian, Germanic, and Walichian influences can be heard.

Although other religious groups, including many Jews, have always lived in Poland, the majority of Poles are Roman Catholic. Most have remained true to their faith, even when it was considered a crime to be Catholic. Their beliefs helped to hold the nation together under numerous partitionings. Even holidays and celebrations are often tied to religious beliefs. It is often difficult to separate an occasion from its religious significance. In 1978, the Roman Catholic Church elected its first and present Polish Pope, John Paul II.

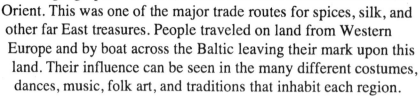

Because of its geographic location, Poland has been a crossroads to the Orient. This was one of the major trade routes for spices, silk, and other far East treasures. People traveled on land from Western Europe and by boat across the Baltic leaving their mark upon this land. Their influence can be seen in the many different costumes, dances, music, folk art, and traditions that inhabit each region.

Poles have always welcomed people of different ethnic groups regardless of race or religion. Constitutions have provided for religious freedom long before the United States Constitution.

Poland is also situated between other powerful countries. In the 1700s, Austria, Prussia, and Russia took advantage of Poland's political weakness and partitioned it between themselves. Austria controlled lands to the south, Prussia controlled the west, and Russia the east. For one hundred and fifty years, Poland was wiped off the map. Its language, traditions, customs, anything "Polish" was squelched, but the Poles were a strong people and in secret, kept their heritage alive.

Poland regained its sovereignty during World War I, only to lose it again to the former Soviet Union in World War II. Throughout Communist dominion, Poles have always kept an independent attitude. This was very much in evidence when its free trade unions called *Solidarność* (sohl-ee-DAHR-nohshch), Solidarity, protested against limits on freedom of expression, poor wages, poor working and living conditions, high prices and shortages. With the fall of the Soviet bloc, Poland today finds itself moving quickly towards free enterprise. It continues strongly in its tradition of openness to new ideas and new peoples.

Polish immigrants were one of the largest groups to come to the United States. The earliest settlers arrived in the New World as early as 1608. Their skills in carpentry and the making of pitch, tar, and glass were in demand. The first Polish American settlement was founded in the mid-1800s in Panna Maria, Texas.

Economic and political conditions in Poland became much worse in the late 1800s. Many Polish immigrants came in search of jobs as the United States embarked on its Industrial Revolution. This Great Immigration took place between 1870-1920. The Polish settlers were attracted to low cost farmland and worked in coal mines and factories, especially steel, iron, and textile mills. New immigrants usually settled where Polish communities were already established. A 1990 census showed that people of Polish ancestry made up the ninth largest ethnic group in the United States. States that have a Polish population of over 500,000 are Wisconsin (especially the Milwaukee area), California, Illinois and New

Jersey. Pennsylvania is estimated to have a population of 882,000, Michigan 889,000 and New York logs in at about 1,181,000. Buffalo and New York City have sizable Polish populations, as do Baltimore, Maryland and Detroit, Michigan. Chicago, Illinois still has the largest Polish community in the United States. Its Polish population is second largest to that of Warsaw, the capital of Poland. In the greater Chicago area, my home, there are estimated to be around 1,250,000 Polish people!

Poles continue to immigrate to the United States, although not in such great numbers, for reasons similar to those of almost a century ago. They want to make a better life for themselves. Throughout the United States, Polish communities keep themselves alive and unified through various organizations and clubs. The Polish National Alliance, Polish Roman Catholic Union of America, and the Polish Women's Alliance are just a few which offer such services as insurance, loans, news publications, Polish dance and language schools for children, and financial support to other Polish organizations in their cities.

Polish immigrants contributed much to the making of Chicago. They worked in the stock yards, heavy industry, and supplied factories with the unskilled labor that was needed. They built solid communities with many churches and schools, hospitals and orphanages. They took an active political interest in the city and helped to lay the foundation for Chicago's infrastructure. If you have a chance to visit Chicago you can find Poles living throughout the city and its surrounding suburbs, but there are two large communities that continue to thrive. One is on the northwest side, around the intersection of Milwaukee Avenue and Central Park Avenue, and another on the southwest side of the city around the intersection of Pulaski Road and Archer Avenue. Immigrants can get along here never having to learn English. You will find Polish churches, bookstores, newspapers, fabric stores, card and folk art shops, overseas delivery services, professional services, and of course, a multitude of delicatessens and restaurants. Nothing tastes better than *kielbasa* (keel-BAH-sah), spicy fresh sausage, *kapusta* (kah-POO-stah), tangy sauerkraut, and *chleb* (hlehb) baked crusty rye bread. The flavors, tantalizing smells and typical appearance remind Poles of their homeland so far away. Any treasure a homesick Pole could desire is close at hand in these neighborhood shops. The old immigrants as well as the new are determined to keep their culture united and alive and continue to pass traditions along to their children and grandchildren.

Polish MUSIC

The Poles are a musical people who are quick with a song. Singing is a natural part of the home. Children first learn folk tunes from their parents and relatives, and more songs when they attend school. Traditionally, Polish folk music is accompanied by whatever instruments are at hand. These are usually instruments that are easy to carry: the concertina, accordion, violin, string bass, clarinet, and trumpet. If none are available, songs are sung a cappella with great gusto.

Imagine a friendly get-together at home. Inevitably, someone sings a song and others join in. There's a concertina in the closet. One of the visitors just happened to bring along his violin and his brother brought a clarinet. There usually is no written music so instrumentalists and singers play and sing by ear, improvise, or simply compose as they go along. The typical accompaniment is quite straightforward with the usual Western harmonization using thirds and sixths, and chords in major and minor keys. (The Pytlik Brothers Folk Ensemble on the companion recording presents several examples of this style of accompaniment.) The players toss off a few familiar tunes to warm up and then the serious music making gets underway. Tables and chairs are spontaneously pushed aside for dancing, and the group might raise the rafters long into the night.

A common misconception is that the polka, as we Americans know it, is an authentic example of Polish folk music. This is definitely not the case. The polka is a dance form common to many ethnic groups, not just the Poles. *The New Grove Dictionary of Music and Musicians* states that the polka is a lively dance in 2/4 time whose origins are unclear. The name "polka" might have originated form the Czech word *půlka* which means "half" (a dance in half time), the Czech word pole which means "field" (a dance of the peasants), or the Czech word *polska* which means "Polish girl." It is known that the polka was adapted from the Polish Krakowiak dance-songs and used in Bohemia as a round dance. It became popular in the 19th century, was first brought to Prague in 1837, and later introduced in Vienna, St. Petersburg, Paris, London, and the USA. Today it is the Czech national dance.

Immigrants from Central Europe came to the United States bringing their polkas with them. Their melodies and styles were thrown into the musical melting pot and evolved into the polkas Americans know today.

Many of the polkas and waltzes that bands play are based on traditional Polish folk melodies, but you will not see or hear these polkas done in Poland. It is true that Poland has polkas, that is to say, lively dances in 2/4 time, but the style of music and dance differs from the polka hops that are done in the US.

Polkas in the United States are truly a Polish-American art form. There are hundreds of polka bands that are kept busy with making recordings and playing at functions. The instruments used in the bands are similar to those used to accompany traditional folk music. There are also numerous radio programs across the country that devote themselves to playing polkas, waltzes, and *obereks*. The polka scene is very popular in Pennsylvania, Massachusetts, New York, New Jersey, Detroit, Milwaukee, and Chicago. My father-in-law is a polka DJ and has his own show, called the Chet Schafer Show, that broadcasts in Chicago. It is the longest running polka show in Chicago—over forty years.

We in Chicago have two types of polka hops. The first dance step is a lively R, L, R, hold, L, R, L, hold. The second is called the Southwest Side Hop because people living in this area of Chicago dance it this way. It is more bouncy than the first. Begin with a very quick preparation hop on the LF, then R, L, R, hold-quick preparation hop on the RF, then L, R, L. Whichever way you do it, it is very aerobic and lots of fun, but you won't see it in my family's home in Poland unless I teach it to them!

Memories of
MY CHILDHOOD

I had two lovely Polish grandmothers. I never knew my grandfathers because they died before I was born. My impression is that Polish women are strong-willed and very sturdy. This must be because they always worked hard in their homeland, plowing the fields and carrying up buckets of water from a well down the hillside. They had a hard life and the lines in their faces reflected this.

Both sets of my grandparents met and married in the United States. *Dziadek* (JAH-dehk) is the Polish word for grandfather. *Babka*

(BAHB-kah) is the correct Polish word for grandmother, but my two older brothers and I had different names for our grandmothers, both the result of childish mispronunciations. My father's father, Adam Kabala, married Veronica Bajor, both from Kolbuszowa. We called this grandmother Boobi. My mother's father, John Owca, from Ryglice, married Apolonia Pankiewicz from Żołków. This grandmother we called Busha. Both were small, thin ladies with gray hair they would fashion into a long braid and pin up in a bun. Whenever they left the house, they wore a floral head scarf tied under the chin. I wear this type of scarf only when dressed in a folk costume, but each grandmother always kept a modest collection of scarves in a variety of colors and patterns in her dresser drawer.

My mother's mother, Busha, lived to be 86 years old. I had the opportunity of spending many of my childhood days with her. She knew very little English and therefore spoke to me in Polish. Much of the

language that I am able to understand, I attribute to her. Because she came from the foothill region of Poland, her speech contained a bit of the mountain dialect. She loved to work in her garden, which reminded her of Poland, and she taught me to identify certain plants by their smell and taste. On my mother's first trip to Poland, Busha asked her to bring back some grain from the family's fields and most importantly, some soil from her homeland. Busha, never having returned to Poland herself, treasured these gifts until the end of her years.

Whenever I went to visit her, there was always a pot of soup on the stove for me. I loved staying overnight with Busha. She had layers of down-filled quilts and pillows on her bed. I'd throw myself into them and sink down into their cool softness. She had a rocking chair placed by a heating vent and in that warm, cozy spot, she would put me on her lap. Busha would tell me stories about her homeland, the people she left behind, the beauty of the foothills where she grew up, and she would sing old songs to me as we rocked back and forth. Once in a while she would stop and ask me if I understood her. Although I never could catch *everything*, I still nodded yes. It really didn't matter if I understood or not, her voice and the melodies themselves painted a picture vivid enough to transcend words.

Here are a few of the things I remember from my childhood that Busha and my mother taught me.

Abbreviations
R right
L left
F foot
H hand
AX alto xylophone
BX bass xylophone
finger cymbals
CW clockwise
CCW counter clockwise

Greetings

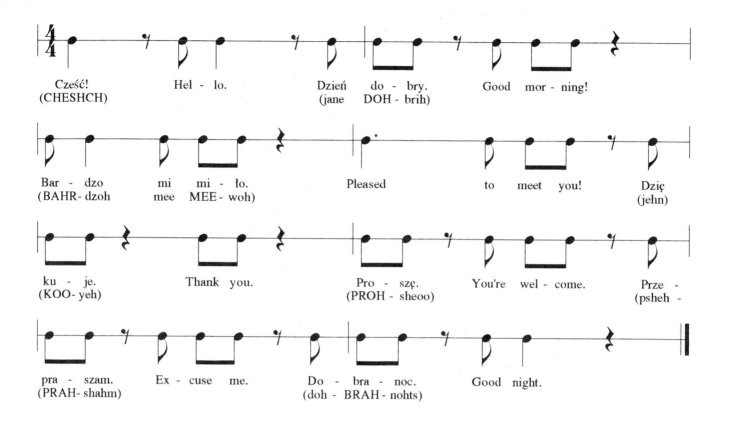

Cześć! (CHESHCH) Hel - lo. Dzień do - bry. (jane DOH - brih) Good mor - ning!

Bar - dzo (BAHR- dzoh mi mi - ło. mee MEE - woh) Pleased to meet you! Dzię (jehn)

ku - je. (KOO- yeh) Thank you. Pro - szę. (PROH - sheoo) You're wel - come. Prze - (psheh -

pra - szam. (PRAH- shahm) Ex - cuse me. Do - bra - noc. (doh - BRAH - nohts) Good night.

© 1995 Andrea Schafer/World Music Press

Two Rhymes

Kotki Dwa

Kittens Two

(Repeat rhythmically while rocking a child)

Ah, ah, kotki dwa
(ah, ah, KOHT-kee dvah)

Szare, bure, obydwa
(SHAH-reh, BOO-reh, OH-bih-dvah)

Nic nie będą robiły,
(neets nyeh BEN-deoo roh-JEE-wih)

Tylko (child's name) bawiły.
(TIHL-koh (child's name) bah-VEE-wih)

Translation
Ah, ah, kittens two,
Both were grey and dark.
They will do nothing
Only play with (child's name).

Tu, Tu, Tu

Here, Here, Here

(You may hold each of the childs' hands in your own to guide the movements)

Line 1: Open one hand. With the finger of the other hand point three times to the center of the open palm.

Line 2: Make circles in the palm, as if stirring porridge.

Line 3: Slap hands together.

Line 4: Grasp each finger, beginning with the thumb.

Line 5: When the little finger is reached, pull up and away, as if to pull it off.

Line 6: Put hands together in the shape of a bird. Make a fluttering motion as the bird flies away, ending with both hands on top of head.

Tu, tu, tu,
(Too, too, too)

Sroczka kaszeczke ważyła.
(SROHCH-kah kah-SHEH-chkeh vah-ZHIH-wah)

Dupke se oparzyła.
(DOOP-keh seh oh-pah-ZIH-wah)

Temu dała, temu dała, temu dała, temu dała,
(TEH-moo DAH-wah...)

A temu małemu łebek urwała!
(ah TEH-moo mah-WEH-moo WEH-behk oor-VAH-wah)

Fyr, fyr, fyr...poleciała
(feer, feer, feer... poh-leh-CHAH-wah)

Translation
Here, here, here
The magpie cooked some porridge.
She burned her bottom.
She fed this one, this one, this one, this one,
And to this little one, she pulled off its head!
Fru, fru, fru... she flew away.

Kołysanka

My memory of when I first heard this song is a bit fuzzy. My mother told me that she and my grandmother used to sing it to me when I was very young. I remember almost all the words and to this day it evokes a warm, comforting feeling when I hear it.

Translation

1. Lullaby my little darling,
Time to hush your cries.
I will rock you very gently
And you close your eyes.
I will rock you very gently
And you close your eyes.

2. Lullaby, now the sun
Says good bye to day.
Night is coming, little darling,
Evening shadows lay.
Night is coming, little darling,
Evening shadows lay.

Kołysanka

(koh-wih-SAHN-kah) - "Lullaby"

Polish Folk Melody
Arranged By Andrea Schafer

Lu - li, lu - li Mo - ja ma - ła czas na cie - bie
(LOO - lee, LOO - lee MOH - yah MAH - wah CHAHS NAH CHEH - byeh
Lu - li, lu - li już sło - ne - czko po - że - gna - ło
(LOO - lee, LOO - lee YOOSH swoh- NEH - chkoh poh - zheh - GNAH - woh

© 1995 Andrea Schafer/World Music Press

Kołysanka

Measures 9-10, partners shake hands

*E*very preschool and kindergarten-aged child in Poland must know this song and dance. In fact, this was one of the first dances I learned while attending Polish language school on Saturdays. It is very simple and quickly learned. It can be done as a mixer (having different partners) or with the same partner. It may be done using all girls, but is more effective using boy/girl partners.

The Dance

Stand in two concentric circles, girls on the outside, boys on the inside.

All face counterclockwise with hands on own waist (girl's L shoulder should be next the boy's R shoulder).

Measures 1-3:
Partners move sideways away from each other (girls to the R, boys to the L) with three sideways steps. On each step, the inside hands make a motion like you are pushing away from each other.

Measure 4:
Stamp with inside foot while placing hand on waist.

Measures 5-7:
Partners move sideways toward each other with three sideways steps. On each step, the inside hands make a motion like you are calling each other.

Measure 8:
Stamp with outside foot while placing hand on waist.

Measures 9-10:
As in photo, shake RH with partner while boy steps to the L and bows, girl steps to the R and curtsies.

Measures 11-12:
Shake LH with partner and step-bow in other direction.

Measures 13-16:
Partners hold both hands (R with L) and walk around each other counterclockwise with four steps to the starting position.

Repeat measures 9-12:
Same movements.

Repeat measures 13-16:
Boys face clockwise, girls face counterclockwise. Take four small steps forward and meet new partner.

Nie Chcę Cię

(nyeh htseoo cheoo) - "Don't Want To"

© 1995 Andrea Schafer/World Music Press

Father Virgilius

This is a circle game that young children in Poland play. It offers the opportunity for movement improvisation. The word "Father" refers to a clerical monk or priest who had a following of one hundred and twenty-three parishioners he called his "children."

Song and Game

Here are a few suggestions for using the game to reinforce specific types of movement. During the B section, tell Father Virgilius you would like to see him/her improvise a movement using
1) a steady beat
2) a high, middle, or low level
3) a dance step they already know i.e. step-hop, skip, gallop
4) a specific quality of movement i.e. smooth, choppy, long, short, fast, slow.

Directions

Teach the A section in English and the B section in Polish. Make a circle holding hands and walk counter clockwise around the circle during the A section. Stop walking when the Polish words are sung. Once everybody is comfortable with this pattern, it is time to demonstrate the game. One person (Father Virgilius) is inside the circle. When the circle stops on "Hejże dzieci," that person demonstrates a movement. The rest of the circle watches and joins in while singing the last phrase of the song. The leader then chooses a new Father Virgilius.

Father Virgilius

"Ojciec Wirgiliusz"

(OY-chets veer-GEE-leeocsh)

A

Fa - ther Vir - gi - lius taught all his chil - dren.
Oj - ciec Wir - gi - liusz u - czył dzie - ci swo - je,
(OY - chets veer - GEE - leeoosh OO - chioo JEH - chee SFOY - eh)

He had one hun - dred twen - ty three chil - dren.
A miał ich wszy - stkich sto dwa - dzie - ścia tro - je,
(AH MEEAOO EEH FSHIH - stkeeh STOH dvah - JEH - shchah TROY - eh)

B

Hey there chil - dren, hey there who do ex - act - ly what I do.
Hej - że dzie - ci, hej - że ha rób - cie to co i ja.
(HEY- zheh JEH - chee HEY- zheh HA ROOB- cheh TOH TSOH EE YAH)

Hey there chil - dren, hey there who do ex - act - ly what I do.
Hej - że dzie - ci, hej - że ha rób - cie to co i ja.
(HEY- zheh JEH - chee HEY- zheh HA ROOB- cheh TOH TSOH EE YAH)

© 1995 Andrea Schafer/World Music Press

Szewc

The game/dance

In this song, the cobbler is fixing shoes and the arm movements resemble sewing and hammering. The dance calls for partners and should be done in a circle. Movements include skipping, kneeling on one knee, and rolling the arms. Learning the dance is an opportunity to focus on form, keeping a steady beat, and keeping your own part.

Formation:
All stand in a circle, partners facing each other

A Section

Measure 1:
Make circles with your own forearms by having them roll around each other stopping on beat 3.

Measure 2:
Reverse direction of arm rolls also stopping on beat 3.

Measure 3 (beats 1 & 3):
Raise arms above head in a V shape.
(beats 2 & 4) Put hands on waist and bend slightly at knees.

Measure 4:
Turn around once, finish facing partner.

Repeat

B Section

Measures 5-8:
Hold partner's hands and skip around each other going clockwise.

Measures 9-16:
Open up into one large group circle, hold hands, and skip counterclockwise.

A Section, measure 1, making circles

"Szewc" is a very simple children's game/dance about a cobbler, from the Warmia (VAR-myah) region of Poland. Shoes are important in country folklore. They were man-made, kept for a long time, and even shared by members of the family. In my grandmothers' time, shoes were a valuable possession. They were repaired many, many times because it was easier to fix an old pair rather than travel by horse-drawn wagon to the nearest town which was miles away. To this day, my mother often includes shoes in the "care" packages she sends to our family in Poland.

Variations to the A Section, kneel facing partner

Variations to the A Section

Measure 1:

Facing partner, kneel on L knee, R fist hits first your own knee, then partner's, then your own again.

Measure 2:

Hit your partner's knee, then your own, then partner's again.

Measure 3:

(beats 1 & 3)

Raise arms above head in a V shape.

(beats 2 & 4)

Put hands on waist and bend slightly at knees.

Measure 4:

Hit your partner's knee, then your own, then partner's again.

Another variation to the A Section

Measure 3:

(beats 1 & 3)

Person #1 raises arms above head in a V shape.

(beats 2 & 4)

Put hands on waist and bend slightly at knees.

Measure 3 :

(beats 1 & 3)

Person # 2 puts hands on waist and bend slightly at knees.

(beats 2 & 4)

Raise arms above head in a V shape.

Other Suggestions:

Have the participants come up with their own movement for the A section. Make sure they can reverse it.
Use a made-up hand clapping game for the A section.
(Challenge: Now reverse it!)

Szewc

(shefts) - "The Cobbler's Dance"

Hey, oh, hey, oh, ha.	Cob - bler has a wire.
Hey, oh, hey, oh, ha.	Cob - bler has a hoof.
Hej - że i no ha.	Szewc dra - tew - kę ma.
(HEY - zheh EE NOH HA.	SHEVTS drah - TEF - keoo MAH.)
Hej - że i no ha.	Szewc ko - py - tko - ma.
(HEY - zheh EE NOH HA.	SHEVTS koh - PIH - tkoh MAH.)

Oo - ha! Oo - ha!	Cob - bler has a wire.
Oo - ha! Oo - ha!	Cob - bler has a hoof.
U - ha! U - ha!	Szewc dra - tew - kę ma.
(OO - ha! OO - ha!	SHEVTS drah - TEF - keoo MAH.)
U - ha! U - ha!	Szewc ko - py - tko - ma.
(OO - ha! OO - ha!	SHEVTS koh - PIH - tkoh MAH.)

Faster

La - la-la-la - la-la-la-la, La - la-la-la - la-la-la-la,

La - la-la-la - la-la-la-la - la-la - la - la - la.

La - la-la-la - la-la-la-la, La - la-la-la - la-la-la-la,

La - la-la-la - la-la-la-la-la-la - la-la - la.

© 1995 Andrea Schafer/World Music Press

Wołtok

"Wołtok" is a dance from Kaszuby in Pomorze (Pomerania), the Baltic Sea region of Poland located in the northwestern part of the country.
The tune, which is in 3/8 time, comes from Sobieńczyce in the Puck Bay and is composed of a slower, twice repeated, 8-measure A melody and a faster, 24-measure B melody.
In the Kaszubian dialect, which often differs greatly from literary Polish, the title means "quarreling waves" and is truly a dance of the sea.
The movements of the slower first part represent the peaceful rolling of waves, while the faster second part represents the rough waters and whirlpools of a stormy sea.

—*Ada Dziewanowska*

A Section, measure 1

Preparation Activities

1) While listening to the music for the first time, sit cross-legged on the floor in a circle. Wait out the introduction. Sway forward on measure 5, sway back on measure 6. Continue this pattern through the entire A section. Find a place on your body to keep a steady beat during the B section.

2) Listen and do preparation step one again, adding the sound of the waves rolling onto the beach. This is made with a "ssssh" sound to every forward sway. Continue to find a place on your body to keep a steady beat on the B section. When the music ends, ask the children how many times the song repeated (it's repeated three times). The form is ABABAB.

3) (This is an important preparation for the A section of the dance.) Sitting cross-legged in a circle, join hands and hold them up with bent elbows. Repeat step two, this time swinging the arms down and forward with each forward sway. Be careful not to bend over too low.

4) Another day, review galloping and skipping. Don't forget to reverse it! Review step-hop and try doing it while turning in place.

The Dance

Formation: Stand in a circle facing center, join hands holding them at shoulder height, elbows are bent.

A Section "Rolling Waves"

Measure 1:
With the RF take a small diagonal step forward to the R, bend body forward slightly and bring arms down and forward as in photo at left, while making a "ssssh" sound (as in Preparation Activity # 3).

Measure 2:
Step behind with LF (do not cross legs) while straightening body and bringing arms up. Repeat pattern for the remainder of A section

The Baltic Sea has been both a blessing and an affliction for Poland. Much commerce is conducted in its port cities, but it has also been the cause of wars. Today, not only are its cities centers for trade and fishing, but the region is noted for its abundant and beautiful amber. During the height of summer, the Baltic Sea attracts vacationers from all over Europe. To be authentic, the dance should be done in trios with the boy in the middle. All trios form a large circle or divide into several circles. For general classroom purposes, I have done this dance all holding hands in a single circle with no specific ordering of boys to girls. It works very nicely this way and the feeling of the dance is not lost.

Variation for B section, no. 3

B Section "Stormy Sea"

Measures 1-7:
Gallop to the side with the RF (7 gallops).

Measure 8:
One step-hop to the side with the RF to reverse direction.

Measures 9-15:
Gallop to the side with the LF (7 gallops).

Measure 16:
One step-hop to the side with the LF to reverse direction.

Measures 17-23: (Same as measures 1-7)

Measure 24:
One step-hop to the side with the RF. Stop with feet together.

Variations for the B Section:
1) Drop hands and skip around the circle counterclockwise. Reverse direction on the eighth measure.
2) Drop hands and step-hop while turning in place for seven measures and reversing direction on the eighth.
3) Assign every two dancers to be partners. Standing with right shoulders together, place right arm around partner's waist, free hand (LH) is on your own hip. While in this position, step-hop forward and around each other for 7 measures. On measure 8, let go of partner and turn half way around using one step-hop. (Now partners' left shoulders are together.) Do the same sequence going in the other direction.

Other Suggestions:
1) Divide the dancers into trios holding hands. During the A section, every other trio bends forward on measure 1. The remaining trios begin on measure 2.
2) Play around with the form. Use the same step for the first and third B sections and a different step for the second B section making your form ABACAB. Try changing the step for each B section making the form ABACAD. (The A section always remains the same.)
3) Older students can experiment with a friend to develop a new step for the B section. The step need not be locomotor. Suggest hand clapping patterns or a change of levels.

Wołtok

(VOHW-tohk) - "Quarreling Waves Dance"

© 1995 Andrea Schafer/World Music Press

Trojak

This is a dance for three people from the coal mining district of Śląsk (Silesia) in southwestern Poland. The story goes that this dance was created because there were fewer men than women, due to accidents in the mines. It is very popular all over Poland and new figures are constantly being added. It is also well liked by children. The melody has two parts: A (slow 3/4 time) and B (fast 2/4 time).

—Ada Dziewanowska

When I attended Polish Saturday school, one of the first dances I learned was the "Trojak", probably because of its simplicity and age appropriate choreography. I also think that the instructors liked it because it calls for one boy dancing with two girls. The girls helped to keep the boy in line and there was always a shortage of boys. This piece is an opportunity for recorder players to work as an ensemble, playing in triple and duple meter.

B Section, measure 1-3

Translation

The mountaineers have sown their oats,
sown their oats,
From one end to the other end,
oh yes, oh yes,
The moutaineers have sown their rye,
sown their rye,
From one end to the other end,
all of it, all of it.

The Dance

Formation: In groups of three, stand in a line facing front. (Ideally there should be two girls with one boy in the center.) Holding inside hands, the girl may hold on to her skirt with her outside hand or leave it on her waist.

A Section (slow and gentle)

Measure 1:
Step on RF and swing L leg gently across and in front. Rise slightly onto ball of RF on beat 2, come down on beat 3.

Measure 2: (Same as measure 1, but begin left.)

Measure 3:
Gently stamp foot, R L wait.

Measure 4:
Gently stamp foot, R L wait.

Measures 5-8: (Repeat m. 1-4)

Measures 9-12: (Repeat m. 1-4)

Measures 13-16: (Repeat m. 1-4)

B Section (fast and lively)

Measures 1-3:
Continue to hold hands. As in photo at left, boy raises L arm with partner on L. Girl on R skips under raised arms, boy also follows through. (He must turn under his own arm to face front again.) Return to place.

*T*oday, coal mining is still the main industry of Śląsk. Approximately 98% of Poland's coal comes from this region. Steel mills, metal, chemical, electrical, and car assembly plants make this area known as the "industrial heart of Poland."

Fortunately, mining is less hazardous than in the past, but industrial pollution is taking its toll on the environment. Poland is just beginning to set environmental standards and pollution controls.

Measure 4 :
Stamp 3 times, R L R.

Measures 5-7:
(Same as measure 1-3, begin with girl on L.)

Measure 8:
Stamp 3 times, R L R.

Measures 9-12:
(Same as m. 1-4.)

Measures 13-16:
(Same as m. 5-8.)

Variations to the B Section:

The variations are endless. Ask for ideas from your dancers as to what they would like to do. Here are a couple of favorites.

1. One-Big-Circle

All three persons make a circle. Using a side gallop step, circle counterclockwise for 3 measures, then stamp 3 times. Reverse.

2. The Cuddle-Up (see photo at left)

Measures 1-2

Boy stands still in the middle of the trio holding partners' hands. Girls roll in to boy (still holding hands).

Measures 3-4

Girls roll out. Repeat this pattern for the rest of the B section.

3. Tug-Of-War

Boy stands in the middle of the trio holding partners' hands.

Measures 1-4:

Girl on the R faces boy and tugs on his R arm with both hands. He and his other partner take a few reluctant steps to the R. During the next 4 measures, the girl on L tugs the boy her way, and so on. It's a fight to the finish!

The Cuddle-Up

Trojak

(Troh-jahk) - "Threesome"

A Polish Folk Melody Arranged By Andrea Schafer • For Dancers And Recorders In Three Parts

Za - sia - li gó - ra - le o - wies,
(zah - SHAH - lee goo - RAH - leh OH - vyes,

o - wies, od koń - ca do koń - ca, tak jest,
OH - vyes,) (OHD KOIN - tsah DOH KOIN - tsah, TAHK YEHST,

tak jest, Za - sia - li gó - ra - le ży - to,
TAHK YEHST,) (zah - SHAH - lee goo - RAH - leh ZHIH - toh,

© 1995 Andrea Schafer/World Music Press

Trojak

ży - to, od koń - ca do koń - ca, wszy - stko,
ZHIH - toh,) (OHD KOIN - tsah DOH KOIN - tsah, FSHIH- stkoh,

wszy - stko.
FSHIH - stkoh,)

Fast and Lively
♩ = 200

Trojak

A Traditional Polish
CHRISTMAS

*S*ome of the most beautiful and beloved of all Polish customs faithfully continued by my family center around Christmas which begins on December 24th and continues through January. The celebration begins on the eve of Christmas with the showing of the first star. At this time, the traditional meatless supper *Wigilia* (vee-GEE-leeah) begins. The table is spread with a white cloth and in the center or under each corner of the cloth is placed a bit of straw. This signifies the Christ child's birth in the manger. An extra place at the table is set for an unexpected guest. There is an old Polish saying, "A guest in the home is like God in the home." First, the oldest person present, usually a grandparent or father, takes a thin Christmas wafer called *opłatek* (oh-PWAH-tehk) and breaks that wafer with each person. Angers are laid aside, apologies are made, and a wish for the new year is given followed by three kisses on the cheek. With his or her wafer, each person then does the same to everyone present.

My family in Poland still symbolically breaks opłatek with us in the United States. In the Christmas card they send, they will include a wafer and wish us many good things, then end with hugs and kisses.

The Christmas Eve meal itself consists of an odd number of courses (seven, nine, or eleven). My grandmother often included the following dishes in her Wigilia: pickled herring, mushroom soup, smoked fish, baked fish, shrimp, pierogi, sauerkraut, potatoes, vegetables, fruit compote, and desserts. After dinner, the entire family usually attends a midnight mass called *Pasterka* (pah-STER-kah).

As generations before me have done, my family sings beautiful carols called *kolędy* (koh-LEN-dih) after the meal and throughout the Christmas season. Kolędy are true folk melodies which are anonymous and might be hundreds of years old. Their beauty is found in the naive simplicity of each melody. It may be surprising, but there is no such thing as a secular Polish carol. All texts are quite religious in nature. The carols describe the birth of Jesus, the star over Bethlehem, the scene at the manger, and the visiting angels, shepherds, and wise men. They usually have many verses and are often based on medieval or folk dance rhythms. They are sung a cappella or can be accompanied by violins, string bass, concertina, accordion, clarinet, trumpet, or whatever combination of instruments are at hand. There are hundreds of these carols and I think that they are the most beautiful in the world.

Holiday Greetings

The following greetings may be heard during the Christmas Season in America as well as Poland!

"Wesołych Świąt"
(veh-SOH-ih shfeeownt)
Merry Christmas

"Bożego Narodzenia"
(boh-ZHEH-goh nah-roh-DZEH-nyah)
God's Birth

"Szczęśliwego Nowego Roku"
(shchen-shlee-WEH-goh noh-WEH-goh ROH-koo)
Happy New Year!

LULAJŻE JEZUNIU

"*L*ulajże Jezuniu," the music for which is on the following page, is probably the most famous of all Polish carols. I learned it at a very young age and have sung it each year since. It is such a simple, lovely melody that it brings tears to the eyes of most Poles. Chopin found the carol so endearing that its theme can be found in his *Scherzo in B minor Op. 20, No. 1.*

Lulajże Jesuniu

(loo-LAEE-zheh yeh-ZOO-nyoo) - "Sleep Little Jesus"

Arranged by Andrea Schafer

© 1995 Andrea Schafer/World Music Press

Lulajże Jesuniu

Polish Mountaineer

A Visit to
THE MOUNTAINS

A raft ride down the
Dunajec River through the
Polish Mountains

Photos Courtesy of Polish National Tourist Office

In the MOUNTAINS

On the southern border of Poland lie the Tatra Mountains which are part of the Carpathian Mountain range. In the heart of this area is the town of *Zakopane* (zah-koh-PAH-neh). It is noted for its beautiful scenery, lakes and valleys, rugged terrain, pristine forests, clean air, and ski and health resorts. People from all over Poland and Europe come to visit this breathtaking place. It is perfect for a family holiday or to stay for an extended period of time. I've had the chance to visit Zakopane on a few occasions and each time I couldn't help but notice the difference in architectural style. The homes tend to be taller than those in the flat lands. They are usually three or four stories high with steep A-line roofs to facilitate the melt-off of snow.

The people of this region are called *Górale* (goo-RAH-leh) which translates to Tatra Mountaineers. They are primarily sheep herders and their main occupation is animal husbandry. They are noted for their woolen fabrics, wood carvings, needle work, and leather making.

Mountaineers dancing

Górale are a very proud people who live through harsh winters and enjoy beautiful but short summers. The region has been exposed to a number of cultural influences, most notably the Slovaks and the Wallachian shepherds. The Wallachian shepherds were a nomadic people who wandered the Carpathian Mountains during the fifteenth and sixteenth centuries and left their mark on the area. Their folklore is still alive and practiced today.

Górale have their own dialect which even native Poles find difficult to understand. Men wear woolen trousers with embroidered patches, fur lined vests over heavy cotton shirts, wide leather belts, and a derby-like woolen hat with an eagle feather stuck into the side. They carry a long handled hatchet called a *ciupaga* (choo-PAH-gah). Its metal edge was sharpened and used as an axe or as a defence against enemies. Its edge has been blunted and is still used in mountain dances and as a walking stick. The ladies wear floral skirts,

Photo Courtesy of Polish National Tourist Office

blouses with handmade eyelet around the collar and throughout the sleeves and cuffs, velvet vests decorated with intricate beadwork which lace up the front with a wide red ribbon, and carry large floral shawls. Both men and women wear *kierpce* (KEER-ptseh), leather moccasins that lace up. My husband and I are wearing this costume in the photo on the back cover of the book.

Folk instruments include the *dudy* (DOO-dih) which are a type of bagpipes, the *geslicki* (geh-SLEE-tskee), a three stringed instrument resembling the violin, and the *piscolka* (pee-STSOHL-kah), a crude wooden fife. Another important member of the folk instrument family is a stringed bass, not necessarily in tune, and played with a bow.

The ruggedness, unrefined, down-to-earth manner of this people have made its way into the music and dance of the region. The melodies are often in the lydian mode, using a raised fourth and full of sharply dotted, accented rhythms. Harmonies are often dissonant with slowly resolving suspensions and cadences. Songs have many verses and sometimes even more are added by singers to whom the song appeals.

The most popular songs are about two different subject matters: the mountain scenery; and songs about a legendary hero, *Janosik* (yah-NOH-sheek), leader of a band of "good guy" outlaws who robbed from the rich and gave to the poor during the seventeenth and eighteenth centuries. Men traditionally sing songs that are in a key which is slightly too high for them and women use a very open throated, chesty sound. The vocal style seems strong, raw and untrained, and those who are good at it add bits of ornamentation. For a trained singer such as myself, this is very hard to do. I find that I have to forget all my classical vocal training, crank-up the volume, and just have fun.

Mountain dances are some of my favorite to perform and watch. They are full of abandon and passion. They are lively, boisterous, and contain fancy footwork. Real mountaineers have very strong legs from hiking up and down the mountains, so men show off their athletic ability by performing lots of squats, kicks, and jumps. Dance steps and musical form are not always set because both dancers and instrumentalists will improvise if the spirit moves them.

Regle

"Regle" is sung by a girl. Imagine her standing in a clearing on a mountain side overlooking a valley. She would sing out strongly, hoping to hear her own voice echo back. The tempo is rather slow and free, holding on a little longer to notes that feel good.

I first encountered an arrangement of this melody in 1985 with the Lira Ensemble. Since then I have come across many different renditions. As in true mountain style, the song is varied a bit by the person performing it. This is my rendition.

Regle

(REH-gleh) - Forests

© 1995 Andrea Schafer/World Music Press

My Harvest Home 49

Zbójnicki

Boys will love this dance! "Zbójnicki" (zbooy-NEE-tskee) is a dance performed only by men. One tries to out-do the other by showing off his athletic ability. A man might even make up a personalized step and do it for only a brief time so that no one else may copy him.

The Zbójnicki walk

Preparation

The tempo for dancing is faster than the sung section. Melodies may be repeated as many times and in whatever form the dancer prefers. The Zbójnicki steps below represent just a few possibilities. Have your dancers come up with their own ideas, as well.

The Dance

A Section

Formation: Stand in a line or semi-circle, holding the long handled hatchet called a *ciupaga* (choo-PAH-gah) straight out vertically in RH. With body erect, place the back of the LH hand on the small of your back, palm open.

While singing, perform this simple step: (Start with feet together.)

Beat 1:
Small step to the R with RF

Beat 2:
LF closes to RF with a weightless stamp

Reverse and repeat this pattern twelve times throughout entire sung section.

B Section

Zbójnicki Walk
(done by the entire group)

Picture someone walking up a steep hill. The upper body is bent foward slightly, steps are very heavy and deliberate. Place the back of the LH hand on the small of your back, palm open, as in photo. The RH holds a ciupaga (if one is not available, the hand is in a fist) and swings back and forth in accordance with the walk. Take one step per beat with each step beginning on a bent knee. The dancers may travel in a circle.

Squat/Kicks

C Section

(may be a solo or done by a few)

Squat/Kicks

Standing front and center, hold ciupaga in RH.

Beat 1: Low squat

Beat 2: Stand, LF kicks up while ciupaga is passed under the leg into the LH, as in photo.

Repeat this step eight times alternating hands and legs.

Squat/Slaps

Standing front and center, hold ciupaga in RH straight out vertically and centered with your body.

Beat 1: Low squat

Beat 2: Stand, bend R knee, pick up R heel in back and with the LH, slap the RF behind the body, as in photo below, transfer ciupaga to LH

Repeat this step eight times alternating hands and legs.

Squat/Slaps

Squats

Squats

Standing front and center, hold ciupaga in RH with LH on small of back.

Beat 1: Low squat

Beat 2: While in the low squat position, put L leg foward

With each beat, alternate legs, bouncing slightly on the supporting leg. Continue for eight measures as in photo.

Split/Jump

Put the ciupaga down and stand front and center.

Beat 1: Small hop on both feet (this is a preparation for the next beat)

Beat 2: Jump high, while in the air open legs wide and bend over to touch both feet

Repeat this eight times.

Ciupaga Jump

Stand front and center. Hold ciupaga in both hands, horizontally, with arms straight down in front.

Beat 1: Small hop on both feet
(this is a preparation for the next beat)

Beat 2: Making yourself into a tight ball, jump through your arms and over the ciupaga so that now you are holding it behind you.

Repeat this eight times so that the ciupaga is behind, then in front.

(This step can also be done by jumping over your hat instead of a ciupaga. Very accomplished dancers might even hold on to the toe of one shoe and jump over that leg.)

Zbójnicki

(zbooy-NEE-tskee) - Outlaws' Dance

* Note: To give the melody a more Lydian flavor, all G naturals may be sharped.

© 1995 Andrea Schafer/World Music Press

Zbójnicki

Solo

(shouted)

Zbójnickiego!
(zbooy - nee TSKYEH - goh)

I, II

B Faster

Recorder

BX

C

Recorder

BX

Recorder

BX

Bringing The
HARVEST HOME

Harvest HOME

Dożynki (doh-ZHIHN-kee) literally means "harvest home." It is the name Polish people give to the many celebrations of the harvest season. Since Poland is primarily an agricultural nation this time of year is very significant—a time of great joy and thanksgiving. Because fields ripen at different times, there is not a specific day on which Dożynki falls. It varies from household to household. Harvesting begins in late August and lasts until November 1. Small towns as well as major cities set aside a day for a parade and other celebrations during these months.

During my visits to Poland, I have seen the men and women in their fields cutting the grain by hand. There are very few motorized tractors even to this day. Tractors are expensive and when they break down, parts are difficult to find. So with a scythe, called a *kosa* (KOH-sah), a long handled implement with a curved blade at the top, the job is completed foot by foot. The grain is piled into small haystacks and left in rows to dry out or loaded onto horse-drawn, wooden carts.

Polish haystacks in August

Many practices, both pagan and Christian, are carried out to insure the best possible results. There are different rituals at specific stages of harvesting. For instance, the cutting of the first grains may be an occasion for a minor celebration including simple food and drink that may be brought out to the field. Toasts are made to the crops and workers, and a glass is thrown to the ground as an offering to the spirits who might inhabit the grain. Sometimes a small band, called a *kapela* (kah-PEH-lah) is hired and the harvesting will start with music.

The last blades of grain to be cut are treated with great ceremony. The harvesters leave an armful of the choicest grain standing. They cut this last and bring it home with music and song. It is bound together and placed on a flat stone along with bread, salt, and a coin. These are symbols of sustenance, fertility, and prosperity. The bundle is then saved and used in the next year's sowing.

Wieniec for Dożynki

When the harvesting is finished, a wreath celebration known as *wieniec* (VYEH-nyehts) begins. Celebrants make wreaths of various sizes, some to wear, some to be carried aloft by a few people. These wreaths are adorned with all that has been grown in the fields, in the orchards, and in the woods, including apples, nuts, grains, herbs, and brightly colored flowers and ornaments. The wreaths are then carried to church and blessed. I saw an example of this while visiting my family in Ryglice. In mid-August I visited their church. The aisles were overflowing with large wreaths ready to be blessed for Dożynki.

After the wreaths are blessed, a procession carries them back to the farms. Participants choose a girl, usually a family member, to lead the procession. Wearing a wreath on her head, she leads the throng to the family house. The procession arrives and the house is doused with water, much of which lands on the leader! This custom is to insure a good rainfall for the coming year. The head of the household takes the wreath from the girl's head and rewards her with money. All are invited inside for food, drink, singing, and dancing. In the days before World War I, when lords owned large pieces of land and hired peasants to work the fields, this was a time for both lord and peasant to celebrate together.

Today, a national Dożynki takes place annually, each year in a different city.

Konopki

"*K*onopki" is a singing game Polish children like to play during harvest time. Its movements imitate the binding of sheaves (a bundle of stalks) which was often the job of youngsters.

Hemp is obtained from the stem of a plant of the mulberry family, and its fibers are used to make cloth and rope.

Fall is the traditional harvest time and is an appropriate time to sing "Konopki," perhaps including it in your Thanksgiving celebrations.

It is also an excellent name game for helping the school year get underway.

The Game

Make small circles of about ten children each.

Each circle holds hands and slowly walks counterclockwise.

A leader (may be the teacher the first time through) stands in the center and very slowly turns in place counterclockwise during the entire song.

The leader will sing out someone's name during measure seven. This new person holds the leader's LH, verse 1 is repeated, and the new person sings out someone else's name on measure seven.

Each new person joins the leader's line in the center which is slowly coiling around itself into a sheaf. When the student named leaves, his or her circle rejoins hands and continues to walk counterclockwise. As the sheaf gets larger the outer circles diminishes.

When everyone is in the sheaf, verse 2 is sung and the sheaf changes direction to clockwise.

The entire class sings the name of the last person. That person leaves to make a new, outside circle moving clockwise.

Continue singing until all the children have been named in reverse order, and are in a large outside circle. At this point the sheaf has unwound itself!

Konopki

(koh-NOH-pkee)

"Hemp" - A Song for Dożynki (doh-ZHYN-kee)

We are har - ves - ting hemp,
Ba - wi - li - śmy się w ko - no - pki,
(bah - vee - LEE - shmih SHEOO fkoh - NOH - pkee)
We are har - ves - ting hemp,
Ba - wi - li - śmy się w ko - no - pki,
(bah - vee - LEE - shmih SHEOO fkoh - NOH - pkee)

But our sheaves are much too small.
A - le ma - my ma - le sno - pki.
(AH - leh MAH - mih MAH - WEH SNOH - pkee)
But our sheaves are much too big now.
A - le ma - my du - żo sno - pki.
(AH - leh MAH - mih DOO - zhoh SNOH - pkee)

Faster

We're too few, we're too few,
Ma - ło nas, ma - ło nas,
(MAH - woh NAHS, MAH - woh NAHS,
We're too many, we're too many,
Du - żo nas, du - żo nas,
(Doo - zhoh NAHS, DOO - zhoh NAHS,

let's have (name) join us now.
więc ty (name) chodź do nas.
VYEHNTS TIH (name) HOHJ DOH NAHS)
let's have (name) leave us now.
więc ty (name) idź od nas.
VYEHNTS TIH (name) EEJ OHD NAHS)

© 1995 Andrea Schafer/World Music Press

The Frog

Żabuleńka

I recently learned this dance at a Polish Folk Dance workshop and had the opportunity to perform it. Although some adults might feel silly performing it, the children love it and the audience has almost as much fun watching it. My first graders are crazy for it!

This is a very simple children's dance from Warmia (VAHR-meeah) region.

Dance in a circle, a semi circle, or in a single or double line.

Partners are not necessary.

The dance may be repeated as many times as you would like.

The Dance

Formation:

Stand in a large circle facing center, arms at your side.

A Section:

On the down beat of every measure, take a small jump forward with both feet and clap once.

Repeat of A Section:

On the down beat of every measure, take a small jump back with both feet and clap once.

B Section:

Choose two children from opposite ends of the circle and have them jump like frogs sideways to the other side. They should jump as high as they can without losing the steady beat. The rest of the circle continues to clap on the down beat of each measure.

On Repeat B Section:

The same children reverse direction and jump back to their original place.

Variations for the B Section:

1) Choose two children to play "Leap Frog" around the circle (using a steady beat of course).

2) Choose two children. As in photo, squat in the center of circle linking R arms. With knees bent, take little hops (one per beat) around each other. On the repeat, link L arms and reverse direction.

3) This is an easier version of no. 2. Choose two children. Hop on RF (one hop per beat) to the center of the circle and link R arms. Continue to hop around each other. On the repeat, hop on LF, link L arms, and reverse direction.

B section variation, squatting in the center

Żabuleńka

(zhah-boo-LAYN-kah) - "The Frog Dance"

© 1995 Andrea Schafer/World Music Press

Dowidzenia

(doh-vee-DZEH-nyah) - "Farewell Round"

By Andrea Schafer

© 1995 Andrea Schafer/World Music Press

Appendix

CRAFTS, RECIPES, PRONUNCIATION, RESOURCES

About WYCINANKI

It is not known precisely when *wycinanki* (vih-chee-NAHN-kee) became an artform. Paper cutout designs appeared in the homes of Polish peasants around the mid-1800s. Freshly whitewashed walls and ceiling beams were decorated with colorful and repetitive designs. During my first trip to Poland in 1971, I had a chance to spend time in the house that my grandmother was born. I remember it having a thatched roof and both the outside and inside were whitewashed in a light blue color. Around the windows and doorways and along the beams were stenciled designs reminiscent of paper cutouts.

Wycinanki were also used to decorate cupboards and furniture. Designs are often symmetrical, rhythmical, and characterized by repeating motifs. There are three common forms: circular, circular with two long strips hanging down, and rectangular. They may be composed of repetitive designs, flowers, trees, animals, people, and other familiar themes. A rooster or hen, like the one pictured on the cover of this book, was a sign of health, prosperity, and that all was well. This became a symbol of good luck. The tools used were those that were at hand, paper and sheep shears. Women primarily did the cutting—probably as a way to entertain the children during the long winter months, so seasonal cutouts naturally emerged. Different regions of Poland developed their own specific style and an experienced eye can tell whether a wycinanka came from Łowicz, Kurpie, Opoczno, Lublin, Poznań, or Kraków.

Today, when visiting Poland, you can find wycinanki in both museums and stores. There are national competitions for artisans and the tourists' demand for wycinanki is great.

Here, Peter shares with you two wycinanki projects. The first is very simple and involves folding a single sheet of paper, cutting, and pasting. The second is more involved using colored paper in a layered effect. Use these patterns to get started, but the real fun starts when you create your own designs.

How To Make Wycinanki Paper Cut Designs

1 Fold a piece of thin black craft paper in half and cut out half of a flower.

2 Using a more lightly colored piece of paper, cut out another half of a flower, making sure that it will fit inside the first flower.

3 Repeat with an even lighter color...

4 ...and once again with a piece of yellow or white paper.

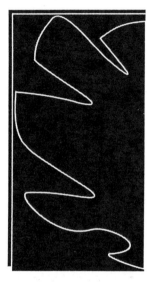

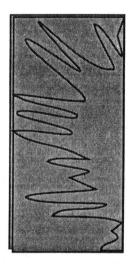

5 Create two identical sets of smaller flowers. One way to do this is to cut both sets at the same time by stacking two sheets of folded paper together.

6 Using black paper cut out the shape of the stem, which will connect the larger flower to the two smaller ones.

7 Unfold and assemble all of the pieces on a backing sheet using rubber cement. This three-part design can also be made with people or animal figures instead of flowers.

A Design Based On The Cover Of This Book

Use a copier to print this pattern on thin colored copier paper. First mask off Side B with a white sheet of paper. Copy the entire sheet on red paper. Then mask off Side A along with the instructions, and copy the entire sheet on a different color paper. Fold the printed pages on the dashed line and carefully cut the images out. Cut details from a third color. Assemble the pieces according to the directions on the previous page.

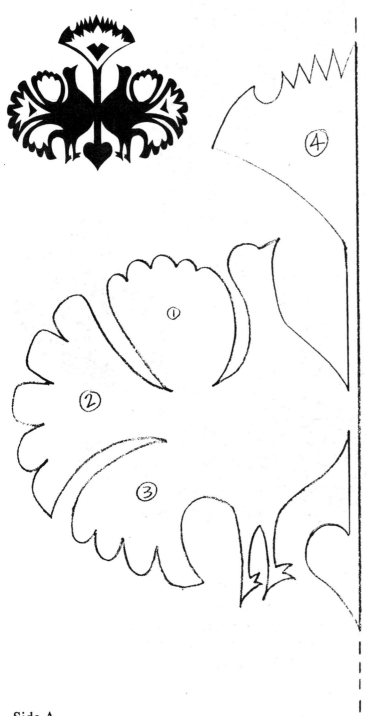

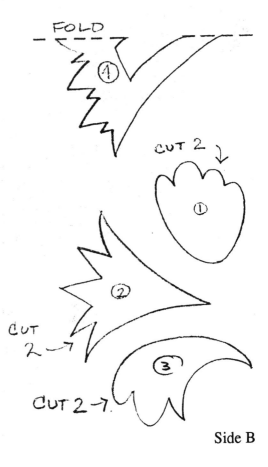

Side A

Side B

How To Fold And Cut A Five Pointed Star

Use a copier to print this pattern on thin colored copier paper. Fold 1 (on dashed line) toward the back. Fold 2 toward the back. Fold 3 forward. Fold 4 toward the back. Turn over and carefully cut out the pattern using sharp nail scissors.

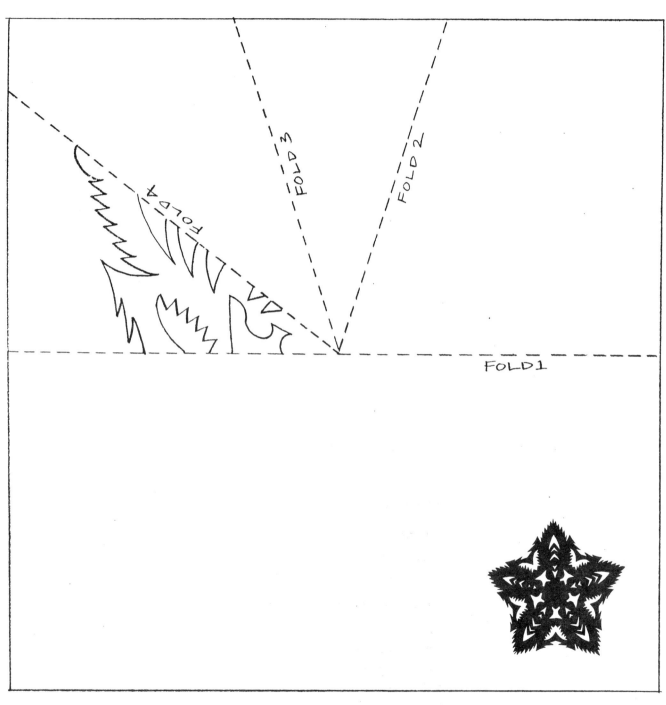

Favorite RECIPES

Here are my three favorite recipes that may be prepared in class or at home. They are very traditional Polish fare, widely enjoyed.

Pierogi

Stuffed Dumplings

(pyeh-ROH-gee)

This can be a meal all on its own. It takes time to make, but is immensely better than the frozen kind from the grocery store. This recipe has been in the family for a while and is quite traditional. If doing this as a class activity, prepare the fillings and dough before hand if you wish.

Ingredients for Dough

2 c all purpose flour
2 eggs
1/2 c water
1/2 t salt

Combine all ingredients in a mixer using bread hooks or mix by hand. Continue kneading by hand until dough is smooth and elastic. Cover dough with a warm bowl and let rest for about 10 minutes. Section off a portion to work with while keeping the rest covered. (This will prevent the dough from drying out.) Roll out dough until quite thin then cut into circles with a 3 1/2 inch cookie cutter or glass. Place a round teaspoon of filling (see below), a little off center into each circle. Wet the edge of the dough with water, fold one half over and press edges together firmly with your thumb or a fork. Make sure the edges are sealed well. Drop the pierogi into salted, gently boiling water and cook for about 5 minutes. Remove from water with a slotted spoon and place in a bowl adding a few pats of butter on top. If you desire crispier pierogi, after boiling, place the pierogi in a frying pan with butter and brown slightly on each side.

Fillings

Mashed Potatoes
Rather stiff. Tasty when mixed with sour cream or shredded cheese.

Sauerkraut (Rinse and chop.)

Cheese
1 c dry cottage cheese (force through a sieve)
1 t lemon juice
1 T sugar
1 egg

Onion and Mushroom

1 medium onion chopped and sautéed
1/2 c mushrooms chopped and sautéed
1/2 c dried Polish or imported mushrooms soaked until soft, then chopped

Meat

1 c finely ground beef or veal
1 medium onion chopped
1 T sour cream
Sauté meat and onion. Add sour cream. Let cool.

Prune

1 c cooked prunes, remove pits
1 t lemon juice
1 t sugar

Blueberry or Cherry

Add a good amount of sugar to the washed fruit (remove pits from cherries) and let it stand for about half an hour.

Other Cooked Fruit

Fruit preserves must be thick.

Bigos

Hunter's Stew

(BEE-gohs)

This is a hearty main course that may be eaten before the soup or as a main lunch-type or evening meal. As the name suggests, it was eaten by hunters and made with whatever the hunt had brought them. It was kept in a pot from week to week and whenever the bigos ran low, fresh ingredients would be added. That way the melding of many different flavors was never lost. This is my way of making bigos. It tastes even better the next day.

Ingredients

28 oz. of good Polish sauerkraut
(Cover with cold water and bring to a boil. Strain off the water.)
1 large diced onion
3 bacon strips
1/2 lb mushrooms sliced
1 handful of dried Polish mushrooms or dried imported mushrooms
(Soak in warm water until soft.)
7 oz. of vegetable stock
2 tart apples diced
1/2 lb of smoked Polish sausage cut into pieces
Your choice of type and amount of the following cut into chunks: potatoes, beef, pork, veal, lamb, venison, chicken

Cut the bacon into pieces and fry in a stock pot. Add the onion and fry until translucent. Add meat and fry until slightly brown. Add all other ingredients and cook until the flavors come together. Salt and pepper to taste. Thicken by adding some corn starch or a bit of rue.

Kołaczki

Kolachky

(koh-LAH-chkee)

This is a recipe made the easy way by using ice-cream. It was given to me by my sister-in-law, Natalie, who is an excellent kołaczki maker. Your kids will love this one!

Ingredients

4 cups all purpose flour
1 lb butter (room temperature)
1 pint, plus a bit more of good vanilla ice-cream
Canned pastry filling (raspberry, apricot, cheese, poppyseed, prune)
Powdered sugar (optional)

Mix flour, softened ice-cream, and butter by hand or in a blender, but be careful not to over mix. Put in the refrigerator to firm up. This step may be done at home if you are doing this as a class activity. The following steps can be done with the children.

Roll dough out onto a floured surface until about 1/4 inch thick. Take a round cookie cutter or glass and cut out circles. Place on ungreased cookie sheet. If the dough gets sticky to work with, sprinkle a bit of flour over it or your hands. Press thumb gently into center of circles. Drop about 1/2 teaspoon of filling into thumbprint. Bake at 375° for about 10 minutes or until just barely golden brown. Let cool. I like mine sprinkled with powdered sugar.

Polish **PRONUNCIATION**

Polish	Phonetic equivalent		International Phonetic Alphabet
a	_ah_	as in _hot_	[a]
ą	_own_	as in _own_	[ɔ̃]
b	_b_	as in _baby_	[b]
c	_ts_	as in _its_	[ts]
ć	_ch_	as in _chase_	[tc]
ch	_h_	as in _hail_	[x]
cz	_ch_	as in _chest_	[tʃ]
d	_d_	as in _dog_	[d]
dź	_d_ followed by a vocalized _sh_		[dʑ]
dż	_d_ followed by a slightly harder vocalized _sh_		[dʒ]
e	_eh_	as in _bed_	[ε]
ę	as in the French words using a nasal _un_		[ε̃]
f	_f_	as in _fast_	[f]
g	_g_	as in _go_	[g]
h	_h_	as in _hail_	[x]
i	_ee_	as in _beet_	[i]
j	_y_	as in _yellow_	[j]
k	_k_	as in _kick_	[k]
l	_l_	as in _let_	[l]
ł	_w_	as in _wet_	[w]
m	_m_	as in _meet_	[m]
n	_n_	as in _no_	[n]
ń	as in _onion_		[ŋ]
o	_oh_	as in _foward_	[ɔ]
ó	_oo_	as in _food_	[u]
p	_p_	as in _pop_	[p]
r	use a rolled _r_		[r]
rz	as in _azure_		[ʒ,ʃ]
s	_s_	as in _say_	[s]
ś	_sh_	as in _she_	[ɕ]
sz	_sh_	as in _ash_	[ʃ]
t	_t_	as in _teach_	[t]
u	_oo_	as in _food_	[u]
w	_v_	as in _vet_	[v]
y	_ih_	as in _sit_	[I]
z	_z_	as in _zebra_	[z]
ź	as in _edge_		[ʒ]
ż	as in _azure_		[ʒ]

* As a rule, in Polish, the second from the last syllable is accented

Selected RESOURCES

Żaba (in Polish), Jan Brzechwa (Nasza Ksiegarnia, Warsaw) 1992

Christmas Decorations, Lester Wegrzecki (28551 San Marino Dr., Southfield, MI 48034) 1987

Cobblestone: The History Magazine for Young People, (vol. 16, # 5 1995)
   (Cobblestone Publishing, Inc. 7 School Street, Peterborough, NH 03458)

Detailed Ancestry Groups for States, (1990 CP-S-1-2)

(66 volumes of unaccompanied regional Polish songs), Dzieła Wzystkie, Oskar Kolberg
   (Polskie Towarzystwo Ludoznawcze, Poznań, Poland) 1982

Folk Dances From Poland vols. 1&2
   Polish National Dances
   Easy Dances From Poland
   Let's Play

   Available from:
   Ada Dziewanowska
   Polish Folklore Researcher and Teacher
   3352 North Hackett Ave.
   Milwaukee, WI 53211

Folk Music in Poland: Songs, Dances, and Instruments: A study of their origins and their development), *Czesław Halski* (Polish Cultural Foundation, London) 1992

Lira Ensemble recordings (order from address below):
   Beloved Polish Songs
   A Collection of Polish Folk Music
   Polish Carols and Hymns
   A Polish-American Christmas
   Sing Along With Me-Let's Learn Polish Together
   Misere by Henryk Górecki
Interview with Lucyna Migala, artistic director and general manager of the Lira Ensemble, 1995
   Loyola University Artists in Residence,
   6525 North Sheridan Road, Chicago, IL, 60626 (312) 539-4900

Lud, Jego Zwyczaje, Sposób Życia, Mowa, Podania, Przysłowia, Obrzędy, Gusła, Zabawy,
   Pieśni, Muzyka, i Tańce (The People, their customs, life-style, speech, folktales, proverbs, rites,
   witchcraft, games, songs, music and dances]
   continued as Obrazy Etnograficzne (Ethnographic Pictures)
   33 vols. by Oskar Kolberg (Warsaw and Kraków, 1861-90/R) 1962-68.

Merrily We Sing 105 Polish Folk Songs, edited by Harriet M. Pawlowska (Wayne State University, Detroit MI.) 1983

New Grove Dictionary of Music and Musicians, edited by Stanley Sadie (vol. 15.) 1980

The Paper Cut-Out Design Book, Ramona Jablonski (Stemmer House Publishers Inc.) 1976

Pieśni Ludu Polskiego (Songs of the Polish People, 41 ballads, 466 unaccompanied dance-songs), Oskar Kolberg (Warsaw) 1857

Piosenki Które Śpiewali Dziadkowie Gdy Byli Mali, Katarzyna Zachwatowicz-Jasieńka, Kazimierz Wiśniak, (copyright by Wydawnictwa Szkolne i Pedagogiczne, Warsaw) 1991

Poland: A Historical Atlas, Iwo Cyprian Pogonowski, (Hippocrene Books, Inc., New York) 1987

Polish Customs, Traditions, and Folklore, Sophie Hodorowicz Knab (Hippocrene Books, New York) 1993

Polish Wycinanki Designs, Frances Drwal (Stemmer House Publishing Company, Inc., MD.) 1984

Polish National Tourist Office in Chicago
333 North Michigan Avenue, Chicago, IL 60601, Suite 224 • (312) 236-9013

Treasured Polish Christmas Customs and Traditions
(Polanie Publishing Co., Minneapolis, MN.) 1973

Treasured Polish Folk Rhymes, Songs and Games (with English translations),
(Polanie Publishing Co., Minneapolis, MN.) 1976

Treasured Polish Recipies for Americans, by the Polanie Club,
(Polanie Publishing Co., Minneapolis, MN.) 1948

Treasured Polish Songs (with English translations), edited by Josepha K. Contoski
(Polanie Publishing Co., Minneapolis, MN.) 1953

INDEX